HIGH-INTEREST STEAM

AUTOMOBILES

Self-Driving

48 mph

HIGH-INTEREST STEAM

AUTOMOBILES

COSMETICS

DRONES

ENVIRONMENT

FASHION

GAMING

MUSIC

SMARTPHONES

SOCIAL MEDIA

SPORTS

HIGH-INTEREST STEAM
AUTOMOBILES

JACQUELINE HAVELKA

MASON CREST
PHILADELPHIA | MIAMI

MASON CREST
PO Box 221876
Hollywood, FL 33022
(866) MCP-BOOK (toll-free) • www.masoncrest.com

First printing

9 8 7 6 5 4 3 2 1
ISBN (hardback) 978-1-4222-4517-0
ISBN (series) 978-1-4222-4516-3
ISBN (ebook) 978-1-4222-7286-2

Library of Congress Cataloging-in-Publication Data

Names: Havelka, Jacqueline, author.
Title: Automobiles / Jacqueline Havelka.
Description: Hollywood, FL : Mason Crest, [2022] | Series: High-interest STEAM |
    Includes bibliographical references and index.
Identifiers: LCCN 2020010903 | ISBN 9781422245170 (hardback) |
    ISBN 9781422272862 (ebook)
Subjects: LCSH: Automobiles–Juvenile literature.
Classification: LCC TL147 .H327 2022 | DDC 629.222–dc23
LC record available at https://lccn.loc.gov/2020010903

Developed and Produced by National Highlights, Inc.
Editor: Andrew Luke
Production: Crafted Content, LLC

QR CODES AND LINKS TO THIRD-PARTY CONTENT

CONTENTS

KEY ICONS TO LOOK FOR

Words to Understand: These words with their easy-to-understand definitions will increase the readers' understanding of the text while building vocabulary skills.

Sidebars: This boxed material within the main text allows readers to build knowledge, gain insights, explore possibilities, and broaden their perspectives by weaving together additional information to provide realistic and holistic perspectives.

Educational Videos: Readers can view videos by scanning our QR codes, providing them with additional educational content to supplement the text. Examples include news coverage, moments in history, speeches, iconic sports moments, and much more!

Text-Dependent Questions: These questions send the reader back to the text for more careful attention to the evidence presented there.

Research Projects: Readers are pointed toward areas of further inquiry connected to each chapter. Suggestions are provided for projects that encourage deeper research and analysis.

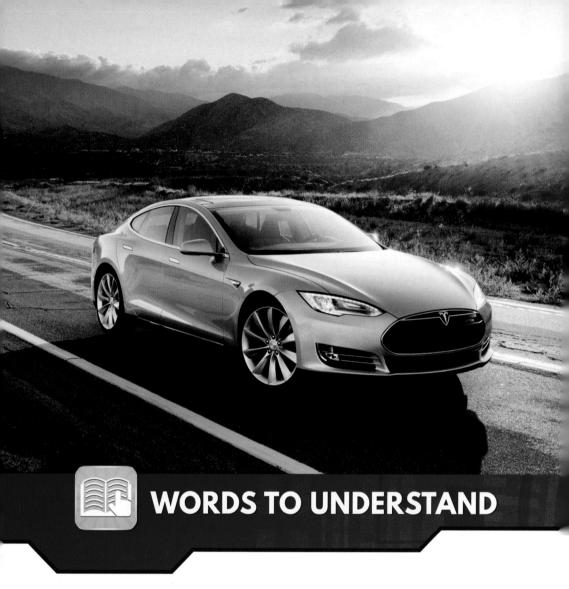

drag force—the force that is opposite to the direction of motion and acting on an object that is moving through a fluid like water or air

horsepower—a measurement of power, where 1 is equivalent to 550 foot-pounds per second, or 745.7 watts

hypercar—a concept car design with an ultra light aerodynamic body made of advanced composite materials

CHAPTER 1

SCIENCE
IN AUTOMOBILES

Mass. Velocity. Acceleration. These are the variables of the science of physics, which is so important to cars. In the days before cars were invented, people had horse-powered transportation—literally a horse-drawn carriage. The 'S' in STEAM is for science, and today, the branch of science called physics has allowed scientists and engineers to create faster, cheaper, and safer cars that are also really enjoyable.

PERFORMANCE VARIABLES

Lots of drivers feel the need for speed. When thinking of a performance vehicle, most people think of a fast car. How do manufacturers make fast cars? What factors influence a car's speed? How have automobile manufacturers used science to advance cars?

Physics in automobiles comes down to two forces: horsepower and drag. These are opposing forces, meaning they work against each other. Even when a car is moving very slowly, some amount of energy is still needed to move the car through the air.

HIGH HORSES

Which car has the most horsepower? It is the Hennessey Venom F5, and it is wicked fast. The Venom F5 is a hypercar that is American-made and has a 1600-horsepower engine that can reach a speed of 301 miles per hour (mph). In less than 10 seconds, the car can accelerate to 186 (mph). Now that's fast! The cost: $1.6 million!

Horsepower measures how much force the engine can apply to a car in a given amount of time, so basically, it is a measurement of power. Car engines are rated for different horsepower, and fast cars with a high horsepower provide much more energy to move the car through the air.

Bigger engines make faster cars, but **drag force** will always be present. Drag is a force that works against motion. It is caused by air friction, and drag is also proportional to speed. The faster a car goes, the more the air works against the car, and that's a drag—literally. Fast cars are designed to minimize friction caused by the surrounding air.

AERODYNAMICS

Did you know there is a whole branch of science dedicated to how air flows around objects? It is called aerodynamics. Fluid dynamics is the more general term, but since air is a very thin fluid, scientists coined the name "aerodynamics." Car manufacturers must optimize airflow around and through the car to maximize fuel efficiency.

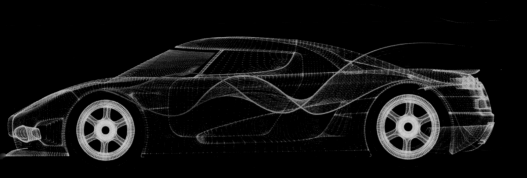

In a car, drag can be further divided into three basic forces: frontal pressure, rear vacuum, and the boundary layer. Frontal pressure is created by the car pushing air aside as it drives. Rear vacuum occurs when air moving around the car creates a hole in the air behind it that cannot be filled. The boundary layer happens where air meets the surface of the vehicle. When engineers understand these three forces, they can describe the majority of car–airflow interactions.

Frontal pressure is created when the air attempts to flow around the front of the car. As the car moves, air molecules are pushed to the front of the car; as they compress, they create pressure. Air pressure is higher at the front of the car and lower on the sides of the car, so frontal pressure is a form of drag.

As air passes over and around the car, a hole is left at the back of the car, and a rear vacuum forms as the air passes through that hole. This space occurs behind the rear window and trunk. Air molecules are simply not able to fill the hole quickly enough as the car travels down the road, and this creates a continuous rear vacuum that forms in the direction opposite of the car. The technical term for this rear vacuum is flow detachment, and it is another form of drag. As the speed of the vehicle increases, the drag increases two-fold.

Open-wheel racecars have large spoilers that disrupt airflow around the car to decrease drag.

Designers try to limit flow detachment by designing the car's contours, tires, and items such as side mirrors to reduce it.

For example, racecars have tails called spoilers that extend beyond the back wheels. The tail allows air to converge more smoothly into the vacuum at the back. When air is able to flow more smoothly, a smaller empty space is created and drag is reduced. The force of the rear vacuum is always greater than frontal pressure, so designers work very hard to minimize the size of the rear vacuum.

A boundary layer is created when the air meets the surface of the car. Depending on the surface, there are two types of airflow and boundary layers: turbulent and laminar. Turbulence is created when air detaches from the car in a rough manner. At the rear of the vehicle, as air finally leaves the car for good, there is an unavoidable turbulent airflow. Turbulent air is chaotic air. Therefore, designers try to create smooth airflow called laminar airflow around the vehicle. Any object that protrudes from a car, like a side mirror or even a hood ornament, can affect laminar flow. If a side mirror were to be designed as a square-shaped object with sharply defined edges, the air coming off

Look under the hood. Your car is a chemistry lesson in the making.

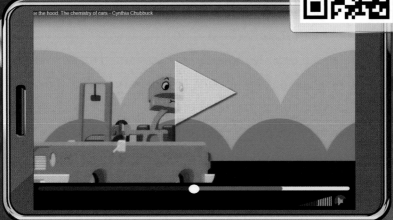

er the hood: The chemistry of cars - Cynthia Chubbuck

that mirror would be turbulent and would also then affect other areas of the car. For this reason, designers create mirrors that are rounded and smooth so that air flows around them in a much steadier fashion. The same concept applies to the wings of an airplane; they are smooth on the front edges so that air flows smoothly over the wing. Designers optimize every aspect of the car to minimize turbulence, therefore minimizing the drag the car encounters.

ENGINE PLACEMENT

You may not think of engine placement as a science, but it is. This placement is a very important consideration in any automobile design, but designers don't choose where it goes. Engines ideally should be as close to the car's center as possible. This scientific concept is a principle of physics, known as center of mass. The engine is usually the heaviest single component of any car, which is why it is best placed in the center. This way the engine itself serves as the car's center of mass.

Forces act on the center of mass, so if the engine is centered, these forces are balanced and are more evenly distributed to the four tires. Imagine having an engine at the very front or very back of the car. When these forces are too concentrated at the front or rear of the car, the tires are more likely to have less grip and will be more likely to slide in turns.

Automakers have over time reduced car engine size while maintaining performance levels. Smaller engines are cheaper, but if they do the same amount of work as a larger engine, consumers are happy. Modern motor oils help coat the cylinders to drastically reduce the friction of pistons so that the engine works much more efficiently.

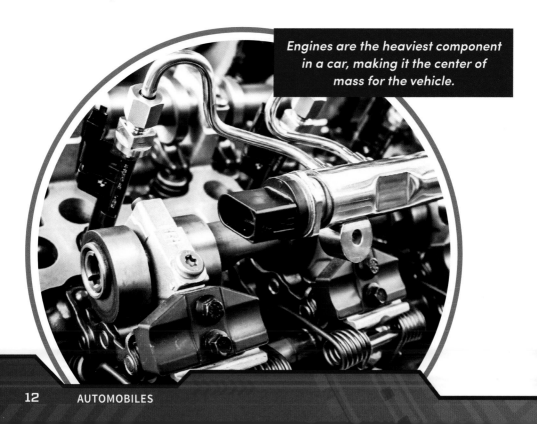

Engines are the heaviest component in a car, making it the center of mass for the vehicle.

Automakers also strive to make the entire car lighter. Scientists use modern composite materials to reduce the overall weight of the car, and designers make the body design more aerodynamic. All of this effort results in less force being required to keep the car moving forward. It's all about physics, and force equals mass × acceleration ($F = ma$), which means $a = F/m$. The lesser the mass, the higher will be the acceleration. A lighter car can move faster, and less force is required to move it.

Think about older cars from the 1950s. These cars were very large and boxy. They weighed a lot and had small engines. As such, they were gas guzzlers. These days the science of physics factors into every aspect of a car's design. Scientists and engineers use the principles of physics to reduce drag, increase horsepower and acceleration, and even to ensure safety.

ENGINE EFFICIENCY

Is it possible for designers to build the perfect car? Can drag force ever be reduced to zero? If it could, the speed of the car would be dependent only on engine power. Can an engine be completely efficient? One of the biggest issues with modern engines is engine efficiency. Most cars have an internal combustion engine (ICE). These use gasoline as fuel, a spark to ignite the fuel, and the engine uses the burning fuel to create power to move the car forward. A simple way to think of efficiency is the ratio of input to output. If all the input fuel was converted to output, the efficiency of the engine would be 100 percent.

Unfortunately, ICEs are not very efficient. In fact, the average engine is only 20–30 percent efficient. Energy is lost as the engine converts fuel. Most of the energy generated by the ICE is wasted as heat instead of being converted into usable energy to move the car forward. Energy is lost in the exhaust and to cooling the engine so that it can run

Internal combustion engines are notoriously inefficient, running at less than 30 percent efficiency.

properly. Friction between the tires and road surface also slows the car down, and that reduces efficiency. If tires had less surface contact with the road, they would be more fuel-efficient, but not very safe. Tires must be designed to compromise between performance and stability for safety. Drag forces on the car also reduce efficiency. The necessity for braking also means that energy is lost to slowing or stopping the car. Energy is also consumed by other parts of the car, like the water pump or oil pump. Adding all of these up means a far from perfectly efficient engine. The highest-efficiency ICE engine invented so far was a 90,000-horsepower diesel engine that was 52 percent efficient.

In 2018, Toyota announced its new Dynamic Force Engine with 40 percent efficiency—twice the efficiency of any other engine on the consumer market. How did Toyota do it? The pistons inside the engine have been specially designed to have a very smooth surface—like a mirror—and that greatly reduces the friction of the piston against the engine cylinder. Toyota scientists also designed a high-efficiency fuel intake port so that more fuel could come into the engine. They also designed a better ignition system to convert more gasoline.

Hybrid engines have both an electric motor and a gasoline-fueled engine.

SCIENCE BEHIND HYBRID CARS

Another way to obtain a more efficient engine is to simply build a different kind of engine, and that is where hybrids come in. What exactly is a hybrid car? A hybrid vehicle uses both traditional gasoline and an electric motor. There are two types of hybrids. The first type uses gasoline to power an electric generator, which creates electrical power to move the car forward. A second type of hybrid plugs in to allow the battery to recharge. When the electric battery is drained, the engine uses gas power.

Both the traditional ICE and a hybrid engine produce horsepower. In a hybrid, though, the traditional gasoline engine and the electric motor share the work of powering the car. Since electric motors are more efficient than gas motors, hybrid cars are more efficient. Most hybrid engines contain the technology that sends any unused energy back to the battery of the electric motor, a key to their superior efficiency.

Hybrids have a large electric motor and a battery pack, which reduce the demand placed on the gasoline engine. This is called

The Toyota Prius is a popular example of a hybrid car.

power-assist science, and it means that hybrid cars can have smaller gas engines that operate at the same or better engine performance. Many hybrid cars can run on an electric-only setting. Since only the battery is driving the car, there is no noise from combustion, which is why many drivers have a hard time adjusting to their hybrid vehicles. When they start the car, it doesn't even sound like it is on.

If you've ever been in a hybrid car like a Toyota Prius and have stopped at a red light, you may have been concerned because the car seemed to have turned off. This is called idle-off capability. The gasoline engine actually shuts off when not in use, like when sitting still at a traffic light. As the driver places his or her foot on the gas pedal to accelerate, the gas engine turns on again.

Hybrid cars also have regenerative braking. As the car accelerates, kinetic energy builds up. As the driver brakes, friction is applied, and that energy is lost through heat in the braking process. Hybrid vehicles have an electric motor that helps recover some of that energy by converting it to electricity and storing it in a battery to be used at a later time.

Modern hybrids also have an extended battery range to increase the use of the electric battery by plugging it in. Plugging in the car and recharging it means an extra 60 miles of power.

ELECTRIC CARS

Some cars, like those made by Tesla, are completely electric. They do not contain an ICE, and therefore need no gasoline, operating completely on battery power. The cars are cheaper to operate and can recharge at home.

The biggest science hurdle for an electric car was producing enough power for long-range driving comparable to a gasoline engine. In a standard car, if the gas tank holds 10 gallons of gas and the car gets 25 miles to the gallon, the driver can go 250 miles before having to stop to fill up the tank.

Tesla cars have long driving ranges. The cars can travel long distances on a single battery charge. Tesla scientists figured out that battery range depended on many factors, so they optimized the car as much as possible. Tesla cars have an energy app that helps drivers maximize efficiency to

Tesla makes cars that run 100 percent on electricity.

Some Tesla models can drive more than 300 miles on a single charge.

maximize range. The app analyzes driving patterns and provides forecasts for when the driver will need to stop to recharge.

The way a person drives and the environment both have a lot to do with the range. If a driver is in a traffic pattern where he or she stops and goes often, this puts a drain on the battery, as does driving uphill because the battery must expend more energy to move the car at a constant speed. Driving into a headwind also drains the battery faster because the car is pushing against the force of the wind, so there is more drag on the car. Likewise, batteries have to work harder in colder weather to keep the car at an ideal temperature. Even factors like tire pressure can affect range. When tires are at optimum inflation, there is less friction against the road surface and thus less drag on the car.

Tesla cars have long-range capability because Tesla excels at making batteries. In fact, the Tesla battery is the most expensive part of a Tesla car. Since the Tesla Roadster was introduced as the company's first electric car in 2008, Tesla batteries have just gotten better and better. Their largest battery pack produces single charge ranges of more than 335 miles.

TEXT-DEPENDENT QUESTIONS

1. What is a performance variable?
2. What is a boundary layer?
3. What is the ideal location for engine placement in a car and why?

RESEARCH PROJECT

Create your own air drag and boundary layer project. While someone drives a car, ride in the passenger seat and safely stick your hand out the window. Make sure there are no trees or objects in your path. Do this on an obstacle-free road. Place your palm in different positions. (1) Hold your arm out, elbow bent to 90 degrees so that your palm is facing inward and flat, parallel with the window. This is the minimum profile for drag. (2) Now turn your palm so that it is facing the oncoming wind. The air pushing against your hand is drag. The faster the car goes, the larger the drag force will be. (3) Finally, place your hand palm down. Now, your hand is an airfoil or spoiler. You should feel the air pushing up on your hand, which will experience lift. Tilt your hand at different angles to simulate the same tilt car manufacturers use on rear spoilers.

WORDS TO UNDERSTAND

aftermarket—after the original sale of a car, there is a secondary market in which owners can by add-on parts

hydraulic—operated by, moved by, or employing water or other liquids in motion

patented—the exclusive right granted by a government to an inventor to manufacture, use, or sell an invention for a certain number of years

CHAPTER 2

TECHNOLOGY
IN AUTOMOBILES

The "T" in STEAM is for technology, and technology has certainly changed since the first car was invented. Since the Industrial Revolution, technology has made a real difference in people's daily lives, particularly when it comes to automobiles. Before cars were invented, people relied on slow and impractical horse-drawn carriages for transportation. Once automobiles were on the roads, technology rapidly progressed to make cars faster, better, cheaper, and safer. At first, only the wealthy could afford cars. Today, we all drive these technological marvels.

HISTORY OF AUTOMOTIVE TECHNOLOGY

Just like the steam engine powered the first train, did you know that the first car ever built was also steam-powered? Although the public didn't like steam-powered cars, several technologies were developed alongside this kind of engine—transmission, steering, and even hand brakes. In 1876, Nikolaus Otto, paving the way for

SCARED OF STEAM

People were very fearful of steam-powered cars when they were first invented. In England, a law required the driver of a steam-powered car to blow a horn and wave a red flag when driving past other vehicles.

the amazing automotive industry, invented a gasoline-powered ICE. This engine offered significantly more power than steam, and pretty soon, the supercharger was invented to give engines even more of a boost. However, the engines were still incredibly expensive.

In the early 1900s, Henry Ford built the Model T, priced at $825 ($21,000 in today's economy). The car had a three-speed manual transmission and a 20-horsepower engine for a top speed of about 45 mph. The car was the first ever affordable car on the market, and Ford sold more than 10,000 in the first year. Even today, Ford's original Model T remains on the list for most-sold cars of all time. Soon after, in 1911, the electric starter was invented, making hand cranks a thing of the past. Cadillac was the first company to use the electric starter in its cars.

Henry Ford is known for introducing the concept of the moving assembly line to mass-produce cars. He introduced mass production in 1913. Before then, each car was individually assembled. With mass production, Ford built cars eight times faster. During the first year, Ford Motor Company tripled its annual production while cutting costs in half. The assembly line meant cars were even more affordable, and average people began to purchase them.

More people driving cars on the streets highlighted the need for more safety. In 1922, **hydraulic** brakes were invented. This technology allowed the car to come to a full stop in much less time compared to hand brakes. To drive

Ford sold thousands of the very popular Model T in the early 1900s.

one of these cars, a person needed to use significant effort to turn the manual steering wheel. The larger the vehicle, the harder it was to steer. In 1926, power steering was invented. A hydraulic system connected the steering wheel to the wheels on the car. The system was too expensive to put into everyday cars, but during World War II, auto-companies built vehicles for the military, which wanted power steering. After the war, in 1951, Chrysler became the first company to put power steering in a consumer car, and other automakers soon followed. Today, every car has power steering.

Think of how chaotic the streets were with all those cars after Henry Ford began mass production. After all, cars did not have turn signals at that time. Finally, in 1925, inventor Edgar Walz, Jr., **patented** a flashing turn signal, but surprisingly, none of the automakers were interested. When his patent expired, Buick introduced turn signals in their new cars and built **aftermarket** kits for cars already on the road.

General Motors built the first automatic gear transmission, which meant that the car changed gears on its own, in 1939.

After turn signals and automatic transmissions, driving was safer and easier, but not very comfortable because there was no heating or air-conditioning (AC). In 1939, the Packard Motor Company offered the first AC system. If passengers got too cold, however, the driver would have to stop

the car, open the hood, and disconnect the AC compressor belt from the engine. Automakers realized how inconvenient this early system was, and in 1953, Chrysler introduced the first dashboard-operated AC system.

It took a couple of decades for cars to become more powerful. In 1957, Chrysler introduced fuel injection to deliver fuel directly to the engine cylinders. These early systems had many problems, and it wasn't until 1982 that Bosch introduced the first fuel injection system that digitally and precisely controlled the air coming into the engine and the fuel delivered to the cylinders. Not only did power improve, but also emissions were reduced.

Safety scored a major win in 1959 with the introduction of the modern seat belt. Earlier forms of seat belts were bulky, and drivers did not trust them. Ford's sales actually declined when they advertised this new safety feature. Volvo introduced retractable seat belts and everything changed; this design is still in use today. In 1971, Chrysler's anti-lock brakes were introduced as another safety feature using computerized controls to prevent skidding when engaged. Other automakers quickly caught on, and by 1985, these brakes were standard on all cars. By 1988, they were offered on motorcycles. Braking systems got an even bigger boost in 1987 when several automakers, including Toyota, BMW, and Mercedes-Benz, introduced electronic stability control systems that applied braking to individual wheels. The technology helps to reduce skidding during turns. BMW was the first to make this feature standard on all cars in 1992.

RECENT TECHNOLOGY

One of the more recent technological advances now standard in cars is airbag technology. Automakers tried for decades to successfully build airbags for cars, but they could never get the bags to inflate fast enough. Chrysler was the first to include driver-side airbags in several car models. Drivers liked the feature, and today most cars contain not only driver-side airbags but also airbags on the passenger side as well as side-impact airbags on the doors.

People over the age of fifty remember driving with their parents, who never went anywhere without a large foldout paper map in the glove compartment. Today we have GPS navigation, introduced in Japan by Mazda in 1990. Mazda used the then-new GPS satellites to map the driver's location. General Motors introduced the technology in American cars in 1995. Now, GPS navigation is extremely popular. Some cars have built-in navigation, while other drivers navigate using smartphones.

In modern cars, airbags are positioned throughout the passenger cabin.

FUTURE TECHNOLOGY TRENDS

Perhaps the biggest future trend in automobiles is the widespread adoption of hybrid or fully electric engine technology. The big practical limitation with most fully electric cars is that the battery capacity is insufficient to hold a charge for a long time. Drivers must drive within a limited range and recharge often. Due to this, several manufacturers have developed hybrid vehicles, a mix of electric power and diesel-fueled power. Drivers can drive 300 or more miles on electric power, then use the diesel tank for longer trips. Fully electric carmakers like Tesla have yet to turn a profit, but as climate change continues to become more of a problem, demand for environmentally friendly options, like electric cars, may increase.

Next-generation brakes are called regenerative brakes. Imagine the energy that is expended when the brakes bring thousands of pounds of momentum to a screeching halt. Engineers have discovered a way to store this kinetic energy and use it later. For many years, trains and bicycles have used regenerative braking, but now some cars do. All Tesla models have it, and the technology is expected to be standard on electric cars in the next few years.

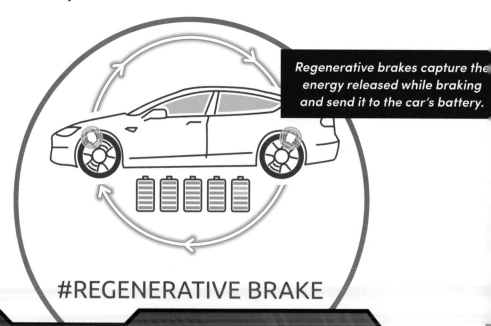

Regenerative brakes capture the energy released while braking and send it to the car's battery.

#REGENERATIVE BRAKE

How about a voice-activated car? American tech company Apple has already revealed CarPlay, which is like artificial intelligence for the automobile. The car's navigation and music are controlled by voice activation. Designers are currently improving on systems like CarPlay to control most of the functions in a car. For example, instead of pushing a button for cruise control, the driver can just say "hold speed at 55 mph."

What if all the information on your dashboard was on your windshield instead? This is called a heads-up display (HUD) windshield, and although it has been available in many models for years, this technology is likely to be a part of most future cars. Designers view the inside of the windshield as "prime real estate," meaning it is an ideally located space that is currently not utilized. Information can be displayed on the inside of the windshield, and the driver can see all data relative to the car's performance without having to take his or her eyes off the road.

SELF-DRIVING CARS

Perhaps the coolest technology trend in the industry is driverless or self-driving cars. This is the future of personal transportation. Cars can already self-brake and self-park, but a completely autonomous vehicle that could operate without a driver behind the wheel is also a reality and may soon become legal on the streets.

What technology is behind a self-driving car? Designers say there are three main technologies: connectivity, software algorithms, and high-tech sensors. Many of the sensors used in autonomous cars have already been developed for other purposes like lane tracking, forward collision warning, and monitoring of blind spots. Designers have added other sensors for radar, cameras, and ultrasound. The next time you see a driverless car, notice the box on top of the car; this houses all of these sensors.

Software algorithms are used to read the data from the sensors. The algorithms then make decisions. Engineers say that these algorithms are

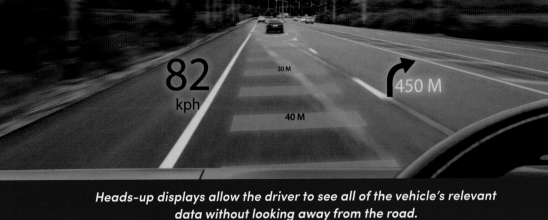

Heads-up displays allow the driver to see all of the vehicle's relevant data without looking away from the road.

by far the most complex because they have to be able to make decisions about many simple and complex driving situations, all at once, and they can't be wrong. Many decisions are at play—everything from speed to route to steering and braking.

Network connectivity is vital in a self-driving car. The car's computer system must have access to the latest road conditions, weather information, traffic conditions, maps, construction areas, and more. All of this data is being used to monitor the car's real-time environment to know the road and know where adjacent cars are.

Driverless cars have a complicated system of sensors and cameras that provide information to the car's computer. Many car companies like Cadillac and Mercedes-Benz began using this technology in 2015 and continue to improve on it. Today, these systems help drivers with roadway awareness and some automated features. The systems are the foundation for future driverless cars.

Many universities are building self-driving cars, and Google and Tesla are the most famous companies that are promoting the technology. Interestingly, they both have taken very different approaches. Google uses LIDAR technology; it is like radar, but instead of using radio waves, it uses light. LIDAR sensors mean that the car does not need foot pedals or a steering wheel. See Chapter 5 for more about the math behind LIDAR.

Tesla's car is more software-driven. The company's Autopilot software uses high-tech camera sensors that serve as the car's "eyes." Autopilot

Texas A&M University has the first self-driving bus in the country. Check out the amazing technology here.

has been standard in all Tesla cars since April 2019. The system uses eight external cameras, a radar system, 12 ultrasound sensors, and an advanced onboard computer to reduce the driver's overall workload. Tesla

The autonomous car is not just a thing of the future anymore. They are already on the streets in some cities across America.

has two Autopilot packages that drivers can purchase: autopilot and full self-driving capability. Under current laws, both require a fully attentive driver with hands on the wheel; the driver must be prepared to take control of the car at any time. The autonomous Tesla car is not street-legal yet, but it is just a matter of time.

BENEFITS OF AUTONOMOUS VEHICLES

Self-driving cars are not affected by the human condition. Drivers can be sleepy on the road and not pay attention. They can be angry with road rage and can also be intoxicated or impaired when they get behind the wheel to drive. The National Highway Transportation Safety Association (NHTSA) estimates that 94 percent of car accidents are due to human error.

Sensors in a self-driving car are always observing the environment, but are never going to be sleepy or angry. The sensors can also simultaneously observe—much better than the human eye and brain—conditions in multiple directions. Therefore, these cars could be an important way to make roadways much safer.

While technologies and capabilities continue to evolve toward making autonomous vehicles a reality, there are some hurdles. Right now, autonomous cars are legal only in a few US states (and only with a human driver at the wheel), as regulators weigh how to best ensure their safe interaction with standard human-driven vehicles.

Many people these days cannot drive because of physical impairment or advanced age. Access to a self-driving car would have a profound impact on their lives.

Driverless cars mean that people will be less likely to own a car. Rides will eventually be low cost and convenient, and many people won't have to spend thousands of dollars, particularly in large cities where driving is difficult and parking is expensive. Dr. Daniel Sperling of the Institute of Transportation Studies at the University of California at Davis says we are definitely moving

While autonomous driving technology has come a long way, there are still things that it cannot detect, such as the instructions of a police officer directing traffic.

to a future where people don't own cars: "You'll have a subscription service, maybe, that emphasizes smaller vehicles, or you might want a cheaper service like a van." People in rural areas will still privately own cars, but the number of people who do own private cars will drop significantly.

Cars won't need to park; they'll be continuously moving, dropping people off and picking people up. City infrastructure will change to accommodate driverless cars. We likely won't need large parking lots or garages. Think of what could be done with that space! There could be more room for parks and trees.

There will be much more focus on pedestrian traffic, to make sure the cars watch out for walkers and bikers. More space on the road might be set aside for pedestrians because driverless cars don't need as wide of a lane. Pedestrians might be able to easily cross streets where it makes sense rather than having to walk to the nearest crosswalk or traffic light. In fact, traffic lights might go away entirely.

Driverless cars could change where people live. Today, lots of people consider living close to work to avoid a stressful commute in heavy traffic. In a driverless car, a person could sleep, read, or work on his or her computer, so people may decide to live where they really want to live, without factoring in their workplace location.

A driverless car could deliver your next Amazon package or the next pair of jeans that you buy online. Rather than customers having to visit stores and businesses, companies are likely to use driverless cars to take goods directly to customers. Wouldn't it be cool to have a mobile clothing store, complete with dressing rooms? Experts say this will likely happen. You can place an online order for several sizes of a pair of jeans that can be delivered to you. The truck pulls up, you try them on, and keep and pay for what you want.

Some businesses like Domino's Pizza are already using the technology. The pizza company has teamed with Nuro, a start-up company founded by two former Google employees who worked on the self-driving team there. Nuro specializes in self-driving delivery. In the summer of 2019, Domino's launched a pilot test project to use six custom-built robot cars to deliver pizza in Houston. Nuro has also been testing its cars to deliver groceries in Arizona.

DISADVANTAGES OF DRIVERLESS CARS

As cool as this technology is, not everyone is a fan. Automotive experts say that currently driverless cars would cost $100,000 to own, a price that is unaffordable for most people. Until car companies can drop the cost, most people won't buy them. Jobs will change; people who drive taxis, Uber and delivery trucks will no longer be needed.

Driverless vehicles may also have far-reaching impacts that are not readily apparent. For example, there will likely be a shortage of donor organs. The US Department of Health and Human Services says 13 percent of donor organs come from people who die in car crashes.

Safety is the primary concern that most people have regarding driverless cars. Autonomous cars still have trouble navigating in large pedestrian crowds and in certain weather conditions. Cars may not recognize construction areas or potholes. One computer malfunction could create a really bad accident. What about software hackers? They could hack in and take control of the car, wreaking havoc on the roadways.

As with any kind of advanced technology, there are a lot of factors to consider. If history is any indicator, a way will likely be found to keep technology moving forward.

TEXT-DEPENDENT QUESTIONS

1. When was the electric car starter invented?
2. What is the difference between regenerative and hydraulic brakes?
3. Name two advantages and two disadvantages of driverless cars.

RESEARCH PROJECT

Have a group discussion about who would be at fault when a driverless car has an accident. Is it the passenger? Is it the car manufacturer? Is it the software designer? Is it someone else? Or is no one at fault? Research your positions prior to discussing so the reasons positions are chosen can be supported. Record the discussion and provide a written summary of the arguments made.

 WORDS TO UNDERSTAND

alloy—a material made when various other chemical elements are mixed with a pure metal element to enhance its properties such as strength

interdisciplinary—combining or involving two or more professions, technologies, departments, or the like, as in business, education, or industry

nanotechnology—building of materials on an atomic scale

CHAPTER 3

ENGINEERING
IN AUTOMOBILES

The automotive industry is under constant pressure to design new vehicle features. Cars need the utmost enhanced safety features and must have better fuel economy while simultaneously controlling emissions. So how do they do it? Much of the innovation in the automobile industry comes from advanced materials engineering.

WHAT IS MATERIALS ENGINEERING?

Materials engineering is also known as materials science. It is an **interdisciplinary** field that is relatively new in both science and engineering. Materials engineers apply the properties of matter to create new materials. Materials engineers can work in a variety of areas, including ceramics, glass science, electronic and magnetic materials, metals, and surface science. In automotive engineering, much of the materials engineering focuses on creating materials that are lightweight but that maintain strength.

From the body to the rims, modern car engineers use aluminum alloys extensively.

Metal **alloys** are made of a mixture of metals. For example, aluminum alloy is a mixture of pure aluminum with other elements such as iron, copper, and zinc that are added to increase the strength of aluminum. Alloys are mixed in molten or liquid form. Aluminum already has great properties such as strength and corrosion resistance, but can be even better in alloy form. Lots of things can be made from aluminum alloys, including pop cans, tanks, and airplanes.

Alloy composition began more than 60 years ago, and today there are more than 530 registered alloys made with aluminum alone. Engineers at big aluminum companies such as Alcoa and Norsk Hydro create new aluminum alloys for many industries, including the automotive industry. Cars used to be made of steel, but aluminum alloys are just as strong or stronger and weigh far less.

Check out the incredible engineering behind the Lamborghini sports car!

...borghini Car Designing and Production | Italian Car | Automobile Engineering | Mechanical

An aluminum alloy made with silicon is used for things such as the external panels on car doors. Engineers at Jaguar and Land Rover use a copper–aluminum alloy that is very strong and allows for thinner and lighter panels. One company actually mixed two aluminum alloys together to make many structural components such as the chassis. The aluminum alloy known as AA6061 is used to make car steering components. It contains aluminum, zirconium, zinc, and copper.

Inner panels of cars are often made of the alloy AA5182, which has high magnesium content. Yet another alloy labeled 3004 is used in truck and horse trailers.

Materials engineers are always coming up with new alloys. Fiat Chrysler Automobiles (FCA) has created a high-temperature

Different types of aluminum alloys are used for different parts of the car, such as this crankcase.

aluminum alloy that is mixed with copper to make engine cylinders. This alloy promises to help produce a smaller engine with the same power. Aluminum–lithium alloys are often used in luxury cars. These alloys were once used in other industries like aerospace and have made their way into the automotive industry. One cutting-edge alloy is called "super aluminum." It is an aluminum alloy with nanocrystals embedded in it. It reduces weight while creating a 20 percent increase in strength.

Automakers say aluminum builds a better car. It increases engine performance, boosts fuel economy, and reduces emissions, and is more environmentally friendly. Lots of cars are made of aluminum: Ford, Audi, Mercedes-Benz, and Land Rover all make aluminum cars. Steel is still widely used, but aluminum is the second

HOW GREEN IS GREEN?

Some experts say that an electric car is not as "green" as it seems. These cars use electricity, which has to come from the town's local electricity grid. If the local grid uses coal to produce power, greenhouse gases are still being emitted. On the other hand, if the local electricity is produced by solar or wind power, the electric car is pretty green.

The most important part of an electric car is its battery, which is made of lithium, a very light conductive material that provides low weight and high energy. Lithium is a rare metal that must be mined from the earth. Many environmental experts complain about the damage these lithium mines are causing. Rare metals like lithium exist in very small quantities and in inconvenient places. That means that a lot of earth must be moved to get just a little lithium. One example is China's Jiangxi rare earth mine, where miners dig 8-foot holes and pour acids into them to dissolve the clay earth to expose lithium.

most used material in car-making today. Aluminum can be recycled so it is more environmentally friendly than steel. About 500,000 tons of scrap auto aluminum is recycled each year. Aluminum can also absorb twice as much crash energy as steel; therefore, designers can make larger crush zones. Aluminum is lighter, so engineers can make thicker panels without adding to the overall weight of the vehicle. In some cars, using aluminum means the vehicle is an amazing 50 percent lighter.

The body of the popular Ford F-150 pickup truck is all aluminum.

For example, the Ford F-150 truck body is all aluminum. Interestingly, this truck is the most popular US model of any vehicle. In 2015, designers were able to cut 700 pounds (15 percent of the truck weight) by using an all-aluminum truck body.

Magnesium is even lighter than aluminum. In fact, it is the lightest metal on earth and 33 percent lighter than aluminum. Magnesium is non-toxic, abundant on the earth, and very resistant to denting. Surprisingly, the main source of magnesium is seawater, so the supply is virtually unlimited. Magnesium can also be recycled.

Engineers at Ford, Corvette, and Jeep use magnesium parts. It is easy to cast or mold into whatever part is needed. Magnesium alloys have the highest strength-to-weight ratio of any structured metal, and they are used to reduce weight. These alloys are frequently used in door frames, seat frames, and tailgates on trucks.

COMPOSITE MATERIALS

Composite materials are also mixtures of separate materials to create a new material that is stronger, lighter, and sometimes cheaper.

Composites are used extensively by engineers in the automobile industry because they offer benefits that other materials do not. These types of materials were first used in a car in 1957. Plastic moldings were reinforced with glass fiber to create glass-reinforced plastic (GRP). Plastic is much lighter than steel, and the glass fiber gave the new material greater strength. Engineers got the idea from trees, which are made of natural fibers and an internal sap or resin. Engineers noted that trees will sway without breaking, even in high winds. They duplicated that combination of strength

Bugatti was among the first car companies to use composite materials to engineer stronger and more flexible components.

and flexibility for the auto industry. At first, composites were mainly used in fast cars by makers such as Jaguar, Bugatti, and Lotus, but are now used in every car as well as boats and planes.

Vehicles such a McLaren race car use a composite body because it can be molded into really cool shapes. Carbon fiber composites are the most often used material for automobiles. Carbon fibers give the material strength while allowing for a light weight. In fact, the market for automotive composites will surpass $24 billion by 2024. Composites are definitely in demand as automakers strive for even more fuel efficiency. Fiberglass is another automotive composite that is widely used by engineers. It is lightweight, low cost, and recyclable.

3D PRINTING

Even cooler than all the advanced materials is the fact that many of these materials can be used to 3D-print car parts. In fact, entire concept cars like the Honda Micro-Commuter can be 3D-printed. Most car companies, however, only 3D-print design prototypes. By having a real 3D model, design time is greatly reduced.

3D printing for mass production is another story. 3D printing is slow, so it is not ideal for the manufacturing line. However, 3D printing can be very useful in a process called remanufacturing. Car manufacturers don't keep parts around forever, and as particular car models get older, the parts are harder to find. Companies don't want to keep a large inventory of old parts, so 3D printing may offer value. If someone needs a part for a car that is 10, 15, or even 20 years old, engineers could just 3D print it.

3D printing is an evolving technology in the automotive industry as engineers continue to find ways to expand its capabilities.

At first, 3D printing was used to print very small complex parts that were difficult to make. These days the automotive industry has many new uses for 3D printing technology. Ford found it could manufacture certain 3D parts in one-third of the time of traditional methods.

Engineers are even looking at 3D printing large metal parts. At some auto shows, certain manufacturers are printing large, full-size parts in real time using metals like aluminum in metal form. Composites are ideal for 3D printing. Printable plastics are reinforced with carbon fiber and glass fiber. Experts say the technology will get better and faster to compete with conventional manufacturing processes. Vehicles are much more likely to have many more 3D-printed parts in the next five years.

THIN BUT STRONG

The latest trend in materials engineering is called **nanotechnology**. Designers are using a material called buckypaper that is a super-lightweight carbon material. Buckypaper is 500 times stronger than steel but paper-thin. It is made from carbon nanotubes 50,000 times thinner than a human hair. The material is being considered for cars, personal armor, and vehicle armor.

FUELS

Of course, to increase engine efficiency, engineers don't only have to look at changing the engine. They can also examine changing the fuel. Natural gas and propane are being increasingly used as alternative fuels. These substances offer several advantages. They are not as flammable as gasoline and are lighter than air. They are not corrosive, and they are non-toxic. They don't contaminate the soil or water. These fuels also reduce carbon emissions. Therefore, they are much safer and more environmentally friendly than petroleum-based fuel sources.

Natural gas burns more cleanly than gasoline and has much lower carbon emissions, meaning they emit far less greenhouse gases. Scientists say that engines operating on natural gas can reduce carbon emissions by 20 percent. The other pros of natural gas include: it is very abundant on earth and, therefore, a large supply exists; it can be produced in the United States, so there is no dependency on foreign oil; gasoline-powered cars can be converted to run on natural gas.

Natural gas is a cleaner burning fuel than gasoline, but is still carbon-based.

So why don't we see more natural gas-powered cars on the road? Natural gas is not always cheaper than gasoline, and the United States still doesn't have a good system of natural gas fuel stations. Big cities like Boston, Los Angeles, and New York have many fuel stations, but smaller cities and rural areas do not. Natural gas is cheaper and cleaner, but not as fuel-efficient. Cars that run on natural gas are also more expensive.

According to the US Department of Energy Advanced Fuel Data Center, there are many alternative fuels either on the market or in development. Here are just a few:

- Biodiesel: a renewable fuel made from vegetable oil, animal fat, or recycled cooking grease; many large cities collect kitchen grease from restaurants and recycle it into biodiesel for use in diesel-powered vehicles
- Ethanol: a fuel made from corn is blended and used with gasoline

Corn is used to make ethanol, a fuel that can be blended with gasoline.

- Hydrogen: a gas used to power emissions-free fuel cells that are already being tested on the roads in California. Buses are projected to be the most suitable mode of transportation for the large-scale introduction of this technology.
- Propane: a gas that is readily available and has been used for many years to power vehicles

Perhaps the most interesting alternative fuels are those made of algae. Yes, algae. There are more than 100,000 strains of algae that are genetically diverse. Chemical engineers can experiment on unique properties of different algae to yield biofuels.

Algae can be 100 times more productive than traditional crops. To make these biofuels cost-efficient, near maximum algal production per acre must be achieved.

Companies like ExxonMobil are experimenting with biofuels. The company's engineers have been working for more than a decade to develop a strain of algae that converts carbon dioxide into huge amounts of fat that can then produce energy-rich biodiesel fuel. The scientists actually genetically engineered the algae to make it produce more fat.

Check out this algae farm that makes biofuels.

gy 101 | Algae-to-Fuels

farms next to power plants that use fossil

Scientists are working on developing a biofuel from algae, genetically engineering the organism to make biodiesel.

STEAM CAREERS

Who wouldn't want to go to work every day to 3D-print car parts or make biodiesel fuels? If this appeals to you, you may want to consider a career in automotive engineering. Today, these engineers are in high demand. In this job, you would be designing, developing, testing, and manufacturing automobiles. You would use the skill sets for mechanical, electrical, software, and safety engineering. The profession is very rewarding, but requires a lot of hard work and dedication.

Algae biodiesel emits far fewer greenhouse gases than gasoline, and it doesn't stress food production compared to alternative fuels made from corn or soybeans. What does this mean? When corn is grown for fuel, it creates competition with growing corn for food, meaning less is available for use as food for animals and people. Algae don't require land to grow either.

To produce these fuels at an industrial scale, ExxonMobil would need to engineer algae with a greater ability to convert the sun's energy into biomass. That will increase the algae's fat production.

Automotive engineers work in manufacturing, automation, and computer-aided design. You could work in safety or emissions research, or on noise and vibration. You might work on engine performance or vehicle dynamics. There are so many choices.

TEXT-DEPENDENT QUESTIONS

1. Name some advantages of using alloys and composites instead of steel.
2. Name some of the benefits of biofuels over gasoline.
3. What skills are important for an automotive engineer?

RESEARCH PROJECT

Design your own composite material. Research what materials you would use together to make a new material? What superior qualities would your new material have, and how would your new material be used in automobile design?

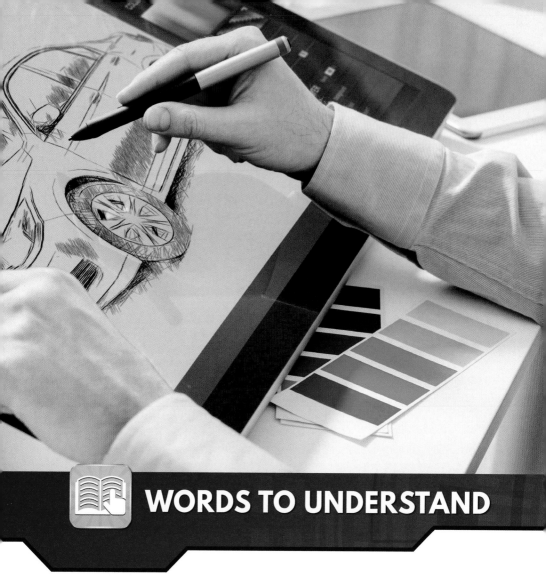

WORDS TO UNDERSTAND

aesthetically—in a way caused by beauty

conceptual design—an early organization or structure of formal elements that has the general idea of something formed by preliminarily combining all its characteristics or particulars of form and function

ergonomics—an applied science that coordinates the design of devices, systems, and physical working conditions with the capacities and requirements of the user

CHAPTER 4

ART
IN AUTOMOBILES

These days, automobile manufacturers face global competition. Long gone are the days of American-made cars being the only cars available for purchase in the US market. There is Volkswagen from Germany, Suzuki from Japan, Peugeot from France, and Hyundai from South Korea, to name a few.

With such stiff competition, these companies are under a tremendous pressure to design cars that are both innovative and **aesthetically** pleasing. This is where the "A" in STEAM comes in, and the "A" stands for art.

AUTOMOTIVE DESIGN

Cars must look nice inside and out to appeal to buyers. To accomplish this, artists and designers have to factor in hundreds of **conceptual design** details. Art has a process, too, from initial concepts to prototypes to design review. The designs must then be evaluated to make sure the car can be manufactured and mass-produced as imagined. Designers must create a concept that can one day become an automobile for sale to the public.

HOW BMW DOES DESIGN

German carmaker BMW has an internal competition to choose new car designs. All the company designers pitch ideas, and the overall winning design is chosen. Once a designer is chosen, there is a years-long design process that BMW follows.

BMW looks ahead to identify future vehicle trends. They are looking far into the future for what buyers will think is modern and cutting-edge. BMW designers look at architecture and fashion to get ideas for future trends. The team has a top-secret group that works on concept cars for the future.

BMW designers say they do much of their work on computers, but consider their hands and eyes to be their two most important tools. The designers begin the competition by producing hand-drawn sketches of the car from many different angles. In the sketches, designers have to factor in safety requirements like wheel base and trunk volume. Any new technology that will be incorporated into the car needs to be visually pleasing and functional.

Next, designers make a tape drawing, a 1:1 scale plan that can be hung on the wall to serve as a map of the future vehicle. In tape drawing,

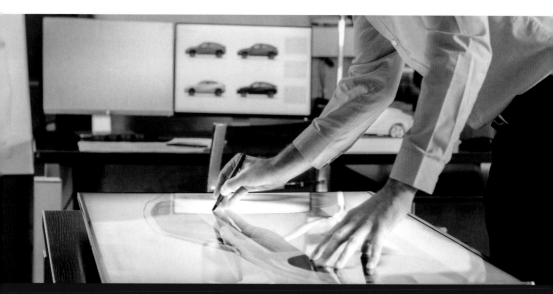

Car designers use state-of-the-art technology to create 3D models of their concepts.

the proportions of the exact vehicle are much clearer; the concept that began in sketches gets much more defined.

Once the tape drawing is finished, designers move on to modeling the car in 3D. The tape drawing serves as the template. At this stage, computer-aided styling designers create a 3D model. The BMW team uses state-of-the-art digital technologies such as virtual reality (VR) headsets to look at the model from every angle. The design process is very efficient this way because VR allows them to see the car in a "living" environment.

At this point, it is time for the designers to make a clay model. BMW says a clay prototype is an essential part of the design process because it will have the exact surfaces, lines, and other details in an actual full-size car. Designers say this is the most thrilling part—when they finally get to walk around an actual replica of the car they've entered into the design contest.

Once the clay model is ready, designers take about a month to assess the lines, surfaces, and proportions of the car to make adjustments. All the clay models for the contest go forward to the decision-making process, which happens about two years before actual production of the automobile. The designs are narrowed down to two finalists, and the BMW Board of Management selects the winner.

CLAY MODELING

In the automotive world, design has definitely gone digital. Designers use computer-aided design (CAD) software, but most cars start out on the design floor using something you would use in your own art class—modeling clay.

Car design is pretty high-tech, but designers consider modeling clay to be one of their most important tools. The clay they use is called industrial clay, and it is widely used in car modeling and by sculptors. Other designers use it to make helmets and even eyeglasses, and special effects artists use it in the movie industry too.

While the computer software can render great 3D drawings, designers say that clay is the best way to physically see the surface of the car. You can actually get a full-time job as an automotive clay modeler! These

Designers use modeling clay to make a physical representation of their designs.

professionals are responsible for taking the designer's sketch and creating a 3D car. By creating a model in clay, designers can look at every angle and design of the car. They can see how light reflects off the surface, and can refine the model for optimal **ergonomics**. Working with clay adds that real touch and feel that is so important to the design.

Before clay is applied, designers use a wood–polystyrene base structure called a buck. Clay modelers then build the model in sections and add clay pieces to the buck. Once the sections are all assembled, modelers use tools to make small refinements like trimming sharp edges or smoothing curves to make the car more aerodynamic. Some modelers actually close their eyes and feel the surfaces of the model to check that it has a smooth surface.

Clay models are done in full-scale, which is called a 1:1 model, meaning the model is the same size as the actual car. The model is then scanned into the CAD software. Clay modelers and CAD designers often work side-by-side to refine the model. Once the

Watch designers from Nissan make a clay car model!

model is complete, a plastic protective layer is placed over the clay and painted to look like a very realistic prototype of the car. The final clay model is covered with a special foil. This makes light and shadow effects visible.

Once complete, the clay model is often re-scanned into the CAD software and converted into a production design.

Students who study car design always take a course in clay model making. These models help the designer understand how to take a 2D concept on paper and turn it into a complex 3D representation. Experienced designers say that without this modeling coursework, clay modelers have difficulty in judging the proportions of a car. Clay is an important tool, and according to designers, clay is here to stay!

SOFTWARE

In the automotive world, design has definitely gone digital. Designers use CAD software like Google SketchUp, Adobe Photoshop, and AutoCAD to create designs. Modern designers use this visualization software to create realistic automobile designs. Designers can quickly and easily produce multiple configurations of one vehicle design, and choose the one they like best.

Visualizing the vehicle from concept to production helps the team make better decisions up-front, cuts down on miscommunication, and speeds up the design process. Prototyping is an expensive process, so using photorealistic visualizations and virtual prototyping, designers can streamline the process and costs. Designers still have to present their designs to the management, who will ultimately decide whether to mass-produce the car, so these visual aids can really help everyone understand what the finished product will actually look like.

With CAD software, designers can easily produce multiple configurations of their design.

VIRTUALLY AMAZING

Car design studios of the future will use cutting-edge technologies like real-time clay modeling, VR headsets, machine learning and artificial intelligence to stay competitive. Computer designs are already so realistic, and the prototypes generated are so lifelike that many of the images you see before the car is for sale are computer-generated images, not images of the real car. Automobile manufacturers used to ship new cars to exotic locations for photo shoots, but today, marketing teams use computer-generated images instead. They can even choose different backgrounds such as the city, beach, or forest for their commercials.

As the design progresses, the team can evaluate the shapes, colors, lighting, and different materials in the design. These 3D models are so sophisticated that designers can even evaluate how different materials will behave. For example, if the team needs to decide whether a part should be metal or plastic, they can design both in the software and determine the most suitable material for that specific part. The software allows the designer to switch environments—let's say from heavy rain to bright sunshine—to determine how the material performs. A white dashboard might look nice, but may produce a heavy glare in bright sunshine conditions.

HOW TO BE AN AUTOMOTIVE DESIGNER

Automobile designers work on the appearance of the vehicle. A designer will typically work on interior design, exterior design, or color and trim design. Interior designers focus on the vehicle interior's function, comfort, and look. They design seats, dashboards, and consoles to be both

Color and trim designers are responsible for the color scheme of the car, including elements like the dashboard and seats.

beautiful and functional. These designers also make sure that buttons and other controls are easy to use and accessible so that they don't affect safety.

Exterior designers work on what the outside of the vehicle will look like. They typically first sketch the design, then sculpt the design in clay. They also use 3D modeling software. Color and trim designers focus on the color scheme of the entire vehicle, both interior and exterior. They develop a color palette for exterior and interior elements like seats and carpeting. They also make decisions such as whether seats should be fabric or leather, and whether to use wood-grain, metal, or other materials for dashboards and other interior elements. Color and trim designers are typically artists who have knowledge of color theory and color mixing.

Automobile design is a creative profession. People must be artistic but also must have great technical skills in CAD software. Designers should have basic drawing skills and detailed knowledge of how cars actually work. They need to know details about the functions of various car parts and how they all fit and work together.

Design schools accept students right out of high school. Students must typically apply for admission to the school and be able to show a portfolio of work. Many design schools offer summer programs for students still attending high school. These programs offer classes that help students prepare to enter the design program. Courses can include 3D design and modeling, sketching, and design theory. In the actual program, students typically take classes in art, sketching, CAD, design theory, physical science, and industrial materials. Students also typically learn about the mechanics of the car, as well as safety standards and other industry requirements. With automobile manufacturing now a global industry, many schools recommend that students know at least one foreign language as well.

Many automobile manufacturers offer summer internships for high school and college students. Design interns usually develop a professional portfolio during their time at the company, and that greatly helps when applying to college, design school, or a job.

CAR DESIGNS OF THE FUTURE

Automotive experts say that major changes to cars happen about every 10 years. Today, designers are creating electric cars and environmentally friendly cars. Imagine designing a three-wheeler car or a car that can go 100 miles on just one gallon of gas. It's happening today in design studios.

Advances in software mean that car companies now take half the time to launch a new design, so it is definitely speeding up the process. Software like Rhinoceros and Solidworks is leading the way.

Today electric cars and batteries, like those in the Tesla, are still an issue because of their weight, but designers say that this too will change. They project that vehicles of the future will be 100 percent green and run on plastic, not fuel.

Future car designs are likely to have a broad and low body (like the 2020 Audi R8) that is lightweight for maximum performance. Having a broad shape allows designers more interior space, and low height improves aerodynamics. This body style has been a growing trend since 2015. Another design trend is a panoramic roof, which is basically an expanded sunroof

The 2020 Audi R8 is an example of a broad, low-bodied car design, which is favored by designers due to the superior aerodynamics and increased interior space the design affords.

with clear panels above all passenger seats. While this concept used to be a safety hazard, glass and high-impact plastics have evolved to now make this possible. Cars of the future are likely to all have four doors, even if the car is very small. Swing-out double doors allow four doors that don't take up additional space. The Honda Element and BMW i3 already feature this design.

Halogen bulbs are still the most common for car headlights, but more cars are likely to use high-efficiency LEDs in the future. LEDs last longer, use much less power, and still provide great light for night driving. Their small size also allows designers to arrange them in some dramatic ways.

TEXT-DEPENDENT QUESTIONS

1. Why do modelers like clay so much?
2. Name two things you will need if you apply to design school.
3. Name three trends that cars of the future will likely have.

RESEARCH PROJECT

Do some research to design your own automobile for the model year 2050. Be sure to include in your design some of the elements cars will likely have or need in the future. Don't be afraid to include elements that might not exist yet. What kind of vehicle will you design—truck, car, or something completely new? What is the most important feature in your design? Explain why you incorporated the features you chose.

percentile—a value on a scale of 100 that indicates the distribution in that hundred that is equal to or below it

proprietary—something that is used, produced, or marketed under exclusive legal right of the inventor or maker

trigonometry—the study of the properties of triangles and related functions and of their applications

CHAPTER 5

MATH
IN AUTOMOBILES

Last but certainly not least, the "M" in STEAM is for math. We use math on a daily basis, whether we realize it or not. We use math a lot when driving: computing distances, computing fuel efficiency—even counting the time spent at a red light, or counting the number of cars on the highway. We use math to calculate tire pressure or the interior temperature of the car, and we definitely use it to calculate speed. Math is truly a universal language. Let's explore some ways that math is used in the automotive industry.

CALCULATIONS

If we know either the engine horsepower or torque values, we can do important calculations.

Torque × RPM / 5,252 = Horsepower (e.g., 415 × 4,000 / 5,252 = 316)
Horsepower × 5,252 / RPM = Torque (e.g., 316 × 5,252 / 4,000 = 415)

Math factors into every aspect of the automotive industry. Car manufacturers want to make a car that appeals to buyers, so they

Aerodynamics is tested with math modeling using data generated in wind tunnels.

start with market analysis. These analysts look at what cars are selling well and how much they are selling for. They analyze market data. They look at factors such as horsepower, weight, and fuel economy to see what buyers are interested in.

Automotive engineers use math every day. Imagine getting the plans for a new body design. The engineer must use intense math to build all the components of the new design. They use CAD modeling software to digitally build the new car. Calculus (and physics) is at the heart of CAD software. Geometry and **trigonometry** are important as well.

Even designing the car's exterior requires lots of math. It's not just about art. In reality, exterior design is a blend of artistry, math, and science. Car designers do sophisticated math modeling in a wind tunnel to determine how aerodynamically air flows around and under the body.

When the car is on the assembly line, math factors heavily into the manufacturing process. Modern manufacturing is automated, and the entire process depends on computer calculations that involve physics, geometry, and trigonometry to determine the best way to assemble components. Manufacturing is a very precise operation, and math is a key to that precision. Manufacturers are also looking for ways in which the manufacturing line can become as efficient as possible. Shaving seconds off an operational step can amount to millions of dollars in savings over an entire year.

Even after the car is built, math can still be used. Product and quality control testing take place. Some cars are sent to the track to be road-tested, and some cars are sent for emissions testing or crash testing. No matter where the production car ends up, math is key.

CAR CRASHES

Car crashes look bad, but there is a whole complex system of underlying mathematics and physics that factor into every crash. Impact forces are extreme during many accidents. Let's use a common example: a 700-pound piano dropped from a height of 50 feet would have an impact force of 12,000 pounds.

A car's mass and speed factor into impact force calculation. Height is a factor in the above piano example, but in car crashes, distance between the two cars, or the car and the object it crashes into, is what is important. How much distance does the impact occur over? This is very important.

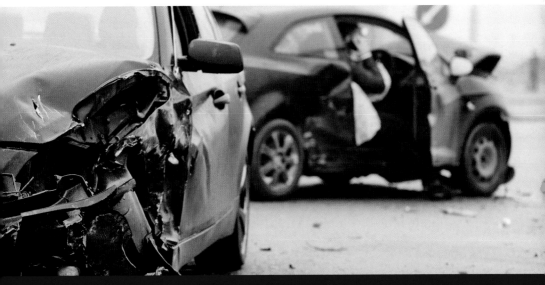

How heavy a car is and how fast it is moving are factors that will increase the force of a crash.

One of the laws of physics is the law regarding conservation of momentum. Most cars have accelerometers, an instrument that can measure acceleration. Since the mass of a car is known, its impact force ($F = ma$) can be calculated. In a car accident, Newton's laws of motion are on full display. Remember that an object at rest stays at rest unless acted on by an unbalanced force (an oncoming car in this case). Also, objects in motion will stay in motion unless acted on by an unbalanced force (like hitting a wall).

Energy transfer occurs during a car crash. The energy from the moving car is transferred to the object it collides with, which may be another car or a wall. The object that is hit either absorbs the oncoming energy or transfers it back to the moving car.

Force and energy both factor in. The car is traveling at a certain speed (velocity) when it hits the wall. The car has a starting and an ending velocity. Acceleration, the time it takes between these two velocities, is important. Not only is the car exerting a force at the wall, the wall is exerting a force on the car.

The energy from the moving car is transferred to the wall. Remember: energy is neither created nor destroyed; it just changes form.

CRUMPLE ZONES

Engineers study the energy of crashes by performing crash testing. In one test, a car going 35 mph crashes into a wall. Test dummies are in the car, and engineers use math to calculate the forces the impact generated on them. Test dummies come in different sizes to simulate males, females, and children. Dummies are placed into driver or passenger positions. They have smart sensors embedded into them to measure acceleration and impact forces. Dummies are built from materials that simulate human anatomical features like

muscle, bone, soft tissue, the brain and other organs. For example, a dummy's spine made of alternating metal and rubber simulates the vertebrae and discs.

Mathematicians use three basic instruments embedded in the dummies to collect data and make calculations:

- Accelerometers
- Load sensors
- Motion sensors

Accelerometers measure acceleration in a particular direction, giving mathematicians a way to estimate the likelihood of injury. Acceleration is the rate of change of speed. A person's head hitting an airbag versus hitting a brick wall both have different rates of change of speed; obviously the airbag is slower so there is less chance of injury. A dummy's head has three accelerometers to measure front–back, up–down, and left–right forces (basically the X, Y, and Z axes). Accelerometers are actually placed throughout the dummy—in the arms, legs, chest, pelvis, and feet.

Load sensors measure the amount of forces on different parts of the dummy body during a crash. Finally, movement sensors placed in the dummy's center of mass measure how much the entire body moved during a crash.

A head-on crash into a fixed object, such as a wall, is a standard crash test scenario.

Carmakers perform several common tests: crashing into a wall, head-on crashes between two cars, high-speed rollovers, and a T-bone collision. Cars tested are safety-and crash-rated. The best cars have a maximized crumple zone to absorb energy.

What exactly is a crumple zone? Also known as a crush zone, it is an area of the vehicle that is actually designed to crumple when a collision occurs. The crumple zone is one of the most effective innovations ever in auto-industry safety.

The crumple zone is designed to absorb the energy of the impact. Basically, the car takes on the energy, so the passengers do not. It takes a lot of math for engineers to design a crumple zone. Keeping people safe is not as easy as it might seem. Engineers must calculate all the stresses of the impact as well as variables like frame stiffness.

At the heart of these calculations, engineers must determine how forces are redistributed when the crumple zone absorbs energy. Most automakers keep their crumple zone designs as **proprietary**, but they do incorporate some common elements. First, the car frame is built to bend a certain way on impact. Second, metals and other materials are actually optimized to absorb as much kinetic energy as possible. Many use a honeycomb design.

A HONEY OF A DESIGN

There is interesting math behind the honeycomb's hexagonal structure. Honeycombs are symmetrical. Mathematicians consider honeycombs to be a masterpiece of engineering. Honeycomb design is an optimal way to cover a large region with small shapes of the same size. The math problem of honeycombs is called the honeycomb conjecture. The comb has an optimal arrangement of equally sized cells with no wasted volume called close packing. The arrangement provides an optimum density. In 1900, mathematicians said the honeycomb conjecture would be one of the strongest influences of mathematical research, and they are right. Today, designers often use the honeycomb structure in designs like crumple zones. Maximum density means maximum absorption of kinetic energy.

CRASH TESTING

The National Highway Traffic Safety Administration (NHTSA) conducts two types of crash tests on every new car. First is the frontal impact test. Conducted at 35 mph (56 kilometers per hour (kph)), the car is driven straight into a solid concrete barrier to simulate hitting another car in a head-on collision. A side impact test is also done at 35 mph. A huge weight (3,015 pounds or 1,368 kilograms) simulates a side collision with another car, such as a car running a red light in an intersection. During both tests, 15 high-speed cameras capture images at 1,000 frames per second to look at the crash from every angle.

Is there a perfect crash scenario? Crashes are all about kinetic energy mathematical calculations. When your car is moving at 35 mph,

Watch how Lexus designs crumple zones.

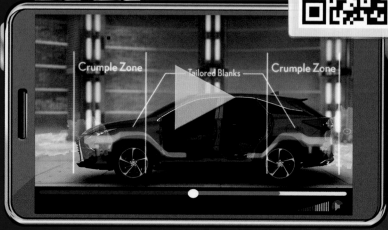

Crumple Zone   Tailored Blanks   Crumple Zone

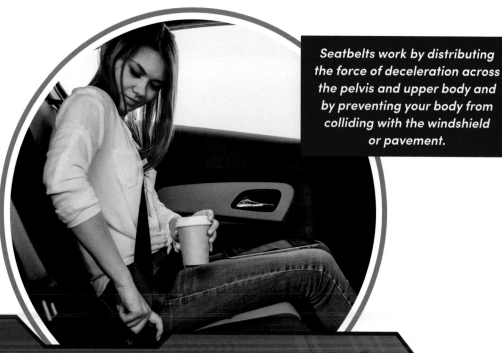

Seatbelts work by distributing the force of deceleration across the pelvis and upper body and by preventing your body from colliding with the windshield or pavement.

so is your body. When the car comes to a complete stop after the crash, you have zero kinetic energy. The best crash scenario is one where the kinetic energy transition from 35 mph to zero happens as slowly and evenly as possible.

The crumple zone definitely helps, as do other safety features such as seatbelts and airbags. Have you ever wondered why the seatbelt tightens up if you suddenly move? By tensing up, the seatbelt can absorb some of the kinetic energy. As the airbag deploys, it absorbs some of your forward motion and, therefore, also absorbs kinetic energy. Cars are designed so that all of these systems work in tandem to slow you down. Seatbelts are the first line of protection, so not wearing one means you have more kinetic energy slamming into the airbag—and that will hurt a whole lot more.

ERGONOMICS

The fact that dummies come in different sizes refers to the science of ergonomics. Dummies of different sizes account for different genders and are referred to by **percentiles**, which ranks them according to size. For example, a 50th percentile male dummy is 5 feet, 10 inches (1.78 meters) tall and weighs 170 pounds (77 kg). Being in the 50th percentile means that the dummy is bigger than half the male population and smaller than the other half.

Ergonomics is the science behind the design and arrangement of people in relation to systems they must use, like the car instrument panel or steering wheel. Ergonomics heavily uses elements of geometry and trigonometry to precisely calculate the location of every gauge, display, and button to be easy for the driver to use.

In cars, everything relates to the human, be it the driver or the passenger. Seat position is critically important. The driver must sit at a proper height and have good posture while seated. The back and legs should be properly supported. Pedals must be within reach and buttons should be too. The instrument panel should be easy to read without requiring the driver to take his or her eyes from the road for long. The driving experience should be enjoyable and not tiring.

These days, cars are so technologically advanced that designing a car interior is much like designing a cockpit. The driver has ultimate control, so ergonomics makes sure that the car is designed around the driver, not the other way around.

What do ergonomics engineers design for? Field of vision is very important. The driver must have the widest view possible, so seat position and height are crucial. Designers strive for at least a 180-degree field of view; even more is better. The driver needs to see his or her surroundings, the road surface, and other cars. Designers optimize field of vision to prevent strain on the driver's neck.

Mirror placement and movement is very important to allow the driver to see behind the car and for peripheral vision. Front-view items like gauges are designed to be within the line of sight, meaning the driver doesn't have to move his or her head to read the instrument panel. Controls like knobs and buttons should be easy to operate so the driver is not distracted.

Quite a bit of ergonomic design goes into the steering wheel. It all involves math and angles. Distance from the driver and tilt angle are both important. A steering wheel that is too close or too far away is tiring. Wrists should rest comfortably and the arms need to be in a position that won't allow fatigue to set in. The driver needs elbow room when turning the steering wheel, so ergonomics engineers need to make sure the seat or other objects don't interfere with turning motions. Even the diameter and size of the wheel are important because both determine how much effort the driver will need to make to steer.

Pedals serve an important function, but there is limited space for them. Again, distance between the pedals and the driver's foot is key to

Why are crash test dummies getting fatter?

Dummies cost about $1 million a piece. They've been used in crash tests since the '60s.

Drivers should have good posture and sit at a proper height when behind the wheel.

make leg movements as comfortable as possible, and the driver should be able to move the seat closer to the pedals or change its height. The driver should never stretch to reach the pedals.

Modern cars need to transmit quite a bit of technical data to the driver. Rather than having numerous gauges, many modern dashboard designs have LED displays as a single screen. Data should be easy to read or scroll through. Designers have to look at factors such as brightness, meaning how the display will look under different conditions like glaring sunlight or darkness. The designer then might decide to incorporate an anti-reflective coating on the screen to help with daytime reading.

Ergonomics engineers even look at factors such as cockpit temperature, airflow, and how heat transfers off the engine. Noise level is important too, so designers look at windows and door design to minimize noise. For a smooth ride, floorboards and seats are designed to absorb the bumps and jolts caused by a rough road.

Basically, ergonomics is employed to ensure the optimal safety and comfort of the driver and passengers.

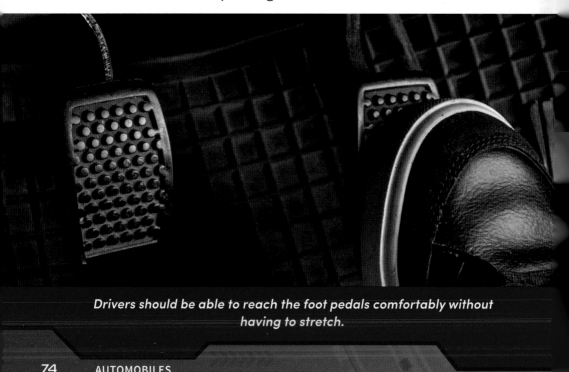

Drivers should be able to reach the foot pedals comfortably without having to stretch.

TEXT-DEPENDENT QUESTIONS

1. Why is crash testing important?
2. Name three sensors that mathematicians use to calculate crash forces in a dummy.
3. What are ergonomic features in the cockpit of a car designed to do?

RESEARCH PROJECT

Research to find some lesser-known safety features and detail three of them in a chart. Explain why you agree or disagree that each feature is helpful or necessary.

FURTHER READING

Auto Editors of Consumer Guide. *Dream Cars: Chronicle of Design and Performance*. Morton Grove: Publications International Ltd., 2018.

Auto Editors of Consumer Guide. *Super Cars: Built for Speed*. Morton Grove: Publications International Ltd., 2018.

Codling, S. *The Art of the Classic Sports Car: Pace and Grace*. Minneapolis: Motorbooks, 2017.

Lasseter, J. *The Art of Cars 3 (Book about Cars Movie, Pixar Books, Books for Kids)*. San Francisco: Chronicle Books, 2018.

Riley, B. *The Art of Race Car Design*. Cheltenham: Icon Publishing Ltd., 2016.

INTERNET RESOURCES

https://sae.org
Society of Automotive Engineers (SAE) International is the global leader in technical learning for the mobility industry.

https://asme.org/engineering-topics/automotive-design
The American Society of Mechanical Engineers (ASME) explores the latest trends in mechanical engineering, including such categories as biomedical engineering, energy, technology and society, robotics, materials, student support, business and career support, and advanced manufacturing.

https://www.energy.gov/eere/bioenergy/algal-biofuels
The Bioenergy Technologies Office's (BETO) Advanced Algal Systems program supports early-stage applied research and development to lower the costs of producing algal biofuels and bioproducts.

https://www.tesla.com/support/autopilot
Tesla, Inc. is accelerating the world's transition to sustainable energy with electric cars, solar panels, and integrated renewable energy solutions.

https://crashtest.org
The crash testing website provides information on auto crash testing, vehicle safety, car safety features, types of car accidents, and accident prevention.

https://www.nhtsa.dot.gov
The National Highway Traffic Safety Administration website has resources and info about staying safe on America's roads.

EDUCATIONAL VIDEO LINKS

Chapter 1: http://x-qr.net/1K4K

Chapter 2: http://x-qr.net/1Lzx

Chapter 3: http://x-qr.net/1Kkt, http://x-qr.net/1KmD

Chapter 4: http://x-qr.net/1Jta

Chapter 5: http://x-qr.net/1KM2, http://x-qr.net/1L6h

AUTHOR BIOGRAPHY

Jacqueline Havelka is a rocket scientist-turned-writer. Jacqueline is a biomedical engineer trained at Texas A&M University. She worked at Lockheed Martin as an aerospace contractor for the NASA Johnson Space Center in Houston, Texas. In her 25-year career, she managed space life sciences experiments and data for the International Space Station & Space Shuttle. She began work on Shuttle mission STS-40 and worked until the last Shuttle launch of STS-135. While at NASA, she served in technical lead and management roles. Jacqueline has been a charter designer of the NASA Life Sciences Data Archive, a repository of NASA human, animal, and biological research, from the Gemini program to the present day.

In 2017, Jacqueline founded her own company, Inform Scientific, to provide medical and technical freelance writing. She has always had the desire to start her own business, and she loves the challenge and diversity of international projects that her business brings. Jacqueline learns something new every single day, and that is a very good thing.

PHOTO CREDITS

DATE DUE
